Nutritious & Nourish

Recipes

Foods to Eat When You Are Sick

BY

Christina Tosch

Copyright Notes

Table of Contents

Introduction

It may come as a surprise to discover that what you eat when you are sick impacts your well-being and recovery.

For instance, for a sore throat, opt for soft foods. When it comes to desserts, choose a frozen treat to help numb and soothe. Recipes including nuts or honey can also assist in reducing congestion.

Oatmeal for breakfast or recipes including eggs are also ideal for anyone to eat when sick.

Is your sick day courtesy of a cold or flu? Then a warming bowl of soup is easy-to-prepare and comforting. Citrus fruits have antibacterial, antioxidant, and antimicrobial properties, which means they are ideal for eating when you are sick.

When it comes to aches and pains, opt for recipes featuring fruits and veggies that are high in potassium, such as bananas and beetroot.

For an upset stomach, banish burgers and fries. Instead, keep it simple; avoid red meat, spicy, and greasy foods.

Are you suffering from a head cold, a stomach virus, or a case of the flu? These 40 nourishing and nutritious recipes featuring the best foods to eat when you are sick will get you fighting fit in no time at all.

Breakfast

Banana Oatmeal

From potatoes to oatmeal, easy-to-digest carbohydrates will become your best friend when you are under the weather. This creamy bowl of oats makes the perfect breakfast to kick-start the day.

Servings: 1

Total Time: 15mins

Ingredients:

- 1 (4 ounces) ripe, black-spotted banana (peeled and chopped)
- ½ cup rolled oats
- ½ tsp ground cinnamon
- A pinch of sea salt
- ½ cup water
- ½ cup almond milk
- Toppings (optional):
- Walnuts, (chopped)
- Blueberries
- Almond butter

Directions:

In a small pot on the stovetop, combine the banana with rolled oats, cinnamon, a pinch of sea salt, water, and almond milk.

Cook the mixture over moderate heat and using a wooden spoon, stirring frequently and mashing the banana as it cooks for 8-10 minutes or until creamy and thick.

Remove from the heat and set aside to rest for 2 minutes to thicken a little more. If you prefer a creamier consistency, you may want to add a splash more milk.

Spoon the oatmeal into a bowl, and add your preferred toppings.

Banana Pudding Jars

If you aren't up to a hot breakfast dish, these no-cook pudding jars are the way to go. Potassium-rich bananas will help strengthen the immune system and boost those flagging energy levels.

Servings: 4

Total Time: 35mins

Ingredients:

- 1 (3.4 ounces) sugar and fat-free instant vanilla pudding mix
- 2 cups fat-free milk (cold)
- 2 small, ripe bananas (peeled and cut into rounds)
- 1 cup granola (divided)
- 1 cup low-fat vanilla Greek yogurt (divided)

Directions:

Add the vanilla pudding mix to a bowl.

Whisk in the milk for 2 minutes until lump-free and homogenous.

Arrange 4-6 slices of fresh bananas in the bottom of 4 (8 ounces) Mason jars.

To each jar, add ¼ cup of granola.

To each jar, add 4-6 tablespoons of the vanilla pudding mix from Step 2.

Finally, top each portion with ¼ cup of yogurt.

Transfer to the fridge for a minimum of 30 minutes before serving. Alternatively, prepare overnight.

Berry-Yogurt Enchiladas

Greek yogurt is tangy and creamy and high in calcium and contains live bacteria cultures to aid digestion. Berries are low in calories but have lots of fiber and vitamin C, and they create the perfect toppings for these breakfast enchiladas.

Servings: 2

Total Time: 12mins

Ingredients:

- ¾ cup fresh strawberries (hulled and sliced small)
- ¾ cup fresh blueberries
- 1 (5½ ounces) container fat-free berry flavor Greek yogurt
- 1 egg
- ¼ cup skimmed milk
- ½ tsp ground cinnamon
- ¼ tsp ground nutmeg
- Nonstick cooking spray
- 2 (8") whole wheat tortillas
- 2 tbsp toasted, sliced almonds
- 1 tsp powdered sugar

Directions:

In a bowl, gently combine the strawberries with the blueberries and Greek yogurt.

Add the egg, milk, cinnamon, and nutmeg to a shallow bowl, and with a fork, whisk until combined.

Spritz a skillet with nonstick cooking spray, and set the skillet over moderate heat.

Dip 1 tortilla into the egg mixture, carefully turning to evenly and well coat on both sides. Allow the excess egg mixture to drip off and place the tortilla in the skillet. Cook on each side for 2 minutes until golden. Repeat the process with the remaining tortillas.

Spoon half of the Greek yogurt-berry mixture in the middle of the cooked tortilla.

Scatter over 1 tablespoon of almonds, and roll up to create an enchilada. Transfer to a plate. Scatter over ½ teaspoon of powdered sugar. Repeat the process with the remaining ingredients.

Serve and enjoy.

Cantaloupe, Papaya, and Kiwi Smoothie

The three fruits combine to create this power-packed smoothie that is great for the digestive system.

Servings: 2

Total Time: 5mins

Ingredients:

- 1 cup cantaloupe (peeled and chopped)
- 1 cup papaya (peeled and chopped)
- 1 kiwi (peeled)
- ½ cup fat-free vanilla Greek yogurt
- A pinch of cinnamon

Directions:

In a food blender, combine the cantaloupe, papaya, and kiwi. Add Greek yogurt and a pinch of cinnamon and process the ingredients until smooth for approximately 30-45 seconds.

Serve and enjoy.

Coconut Water and Lemon Oats

Are you running a fever, vomiting, or sweating? If so, coconut water is the ideal beverage. It's electrolyte-rich and will help to replenish lost fluids. If you are looking for a quick energy boost, use it as an ingredient for this oat breakfast dish.

Servings: 1

Total Time: 4mins

Ingredients:

- 1½ cups rolled oats
- 1½ cups coconut water
- 1 tbsp chia seeds
- Zest of 1 lemon
- 2 drops lemon essential oil
- ¼ cup coconut (shredded)
- 1 tbsp rice malt syrup
- Coconut yogurt (to top)
- Lemon zest (to garnish)

Directions:

In a breakfast bowl, combine the rolled oats with coconut water, chia seeds, lemon zest, essential oil, shredded coconut, and malt syrup.

Top with coconut yogurt and lemon zest, and enjoy.

Eggs Benedict with Yogurt Hollandaise-Style Sauce

A protein-rich breakfast is the best way to set you on the road to recovery. Here, Greek yogurt provides the base for this healthy Hollandaise-style sauce to serve over whole wheat muffins topped with poached eggs and Canadian bacon.

Servings: 2

Total Time: 15mins

Ingredients:

- 2 whole wheat English-style muffins (split)
- 4 thin-cut Canadian bacon slices
- 5 large eggs (divided)
- 1 tbsp butter
- ¾ cup low-fat, plain Greek yogurt
- 1 tbsp mayonnaise
- 1 tsp freshly squeezed lemon juice
- ½ tsp sea salt
- Freshly ground black pepper (as needed)
- 3 tbsp flat-leaf parsley (coarsely chopped)

Directions:

Preheat the main oven to 395 degrees F.

Toast the split muffins, transfer to 2 plates, and keep warm in the preheated oven.

In a frying pan, over medium heat, brown the bacon on both sides for a total of 4 minutes.

Add 1 slice of bacon to each muffin half, and return to the oven to keep warm.

Lightly poach 4 eggs.

Over low heat, in a small pan, melt the butter.

In the meantime, in a bowl, whisk the Greek yogurt with mayonnaise, fresh lemon juice, and the remaining egg. Season the yogurt mixture with salt.

Gradually whisk the Greek yogurt mixture into the melted butter, and heat through until warm. You will need to frequently whisk for around 25 seconds while taking care not to overcook and curdle the sauce.

Remove the muffins from the oven, and top with poached eggs and yogurt sauce.

Season with freshly ground pepper and garnish with chopped parsley.

Garlic Fried Eggs

Garlic has an antimicrobial compound, and according to research, it may help fight bacteria and viruses. Serve it with a vitamin D-rich sunny-side-up egg and enjoy.

Servings: 1

Total Time: 10mins

Ingredients:

- Nonstick cooking spray
- 1 tbsp garlic (peeled and minced)
- 1 tbsp freshly squeezed lemon juice
- 2 eggs
- ¼ tsp salt
- ¼ tsp freshly ground black pepper
- 1 tsp fresh parsley (finely chopped)

Directions:

Spritz a frying pan with nonstick spray and set over moderate heat,

Add the garlic and fresh lemon juice to the pan and sauté for around 2 minutes, taking care not to burn the garlic.

Break the eggs into the frying pan, season with salt and black pepper, and cook for approximately 2 minutes or until the yolks get a little bit firm.

Flip the eggs carefully over, and season once more with salt and black pepper. Cook for 1-2 minutes, depending on how firm you like your egg yolk.

Remove the eggs from the pan, garnish with parsley and enjoy.

Granola, Coconut Yogurt Berry-Nice Cups

These granola breakfast cups filled with coconut yogurt and antioxidant-rich fresh berries are just what doctors order!

Servings: 6

Total Time: 25mins

Ingredients:

- 1½ cups rolled oats
- 1 cup shredded coconut
- ⅓ cup rice malt syrup
- ½ tsp cinnamon
- 2 tsp coconut oil (optional)
- 1 cup coconut yogurt
- Fresh berries of choice

Directions:

Preheat the main oven to 355 degrees F.

In a food blender or processor, combine the oats, shredded coconut, syrup, cinnamon, and coconut oil. On high, process until combined, crumbly and sticky.

Cut ⅓" strips of parchment paper. Place the paper strips inside 6-mini muffin or tart cups.

Spoon the mixture into the 6 cups, pressing it around the sides and leaving space in the middle for the filling.

Bake in the oven until lightly golden for 8-10 minutes.

Remove from the oven, and allow to rest and set for 5 minutes. Then, transfer the cooled cups to a wire baking rack.

When the cups are entirely cool, fill the middles with yogurt and top with berries.

Lemon, Ginger, and Coconut Cookies

Ginger has many amazing health benefits and is an excellent addition to all sorts of recipes, sweet and savory. Combined here with vitamin C-rich lemon juice and zest, these chewy cookies are a go-to breakfast nibble.

Servings: 24

Total Time: 1hr

Ingredients:

- 1 cup unsweetened toasted coconut
- ½ cup unsalted butter
- ½ cup sugar
- 1 egg
- 2 tbsp freshly squeezed lemon juice
- 1 tbsp fresh ginger (peeled and grated)
- 1 tbsp lemon zest
- ½ tsp bicarbonate of soda
- 1¼ cups flour

Directions:

Preheat the main oven to 355 degrees F.

Spread the toasted coconut on a baking sheet, and bake the coconut for 5-10 minutes until the edges are browned lightly. Remove from the oven, and set to one side in a bowl.

Using an electric mixer, cream the butter with the sugar until fluffy and light.

Add the egg, fresh lemon juice, ginger, and lemon zest to the mixer, and mix until silky smooth.

In a bowl, sift the flour with the bicarbonate of soda, and sift into the butter mixture until thoroughly blended.

Cover the bowl, and chill for a minimum of 30 minutes.

In tablespoonful-size balls, scoop out the mixture and roll in the toasted coconut from Step 2.

Arrange the balls, a minimum of 2" apart, on a lightly greased baking sheet.

Bake in the oven for 10-12 minutes until browned lightly on the edges.

Remove the cookies from the oven and set aside to cool on a worktop.

Serve and enjoy.

Lime-Infused Avocado and Egg on Toast

Avocadoes are rich in fiber, healthy fats, vitamins, and minerals. Better yet, they are easy to eat and may help to reduce inflammation.

Servings: 1

Total Time: 8mins

Ingredients:

- 2 fried eggs, sunny-side-up
- 2 wholegrain bread slices (toasted)
- 1 small avocado (peeled, pitted, and mashed)
- 1 tsp freshly squeezed lime juice
- Sea salt and freshly ground black pepper (to season)

Directions:

Prepare the fried eggs, and toast the bread.

In a small bowl, combine the mashed avocado with the fresh lime juice, and season with sea salt and black pepper.

Spread the avocado mixture evenly onto each slice of toasted bread. Top with a sunny-side-up egg, and enjoy.

Red Bell Pepper Omelet

It isn't just a fruit that can claim to be a good source of vitamin C! For example, half a cup of chopped red bell pepper provides around 159% of your vitamin C and 47% of your daily recommended intake of vitamin A.

Servings: 2

Total Time: 20mins

Ingredients:

- Nonstick cooking spray
- 3 eggs
- 3 tbsp water
- ¼ tsp salt
- ⅛ tsp black pepper
- ½ cup red bell pepper (chopped and divided)
- ¼ cup Muenster cheese (shredded and divided)
- 2 green onions (chopped and divided)

Directions:

Spritz an 8" skillet with nonstick cooking spray.

Set the pan over moderate heat.

In a bowl, whisk the eggs with water, salt, and black pepper.

Pour half of the egg mixture into the skillet. The mixture will at once set at the edges. As this happens, push the cooked edges towards the middle, allowing the uncooked egg to flow underneath. Once the eggs are set, add ¼ cup of red bell peppers to one side of the omelet, followed by half of the cheese and half of the green onions. Fold the other side over to cover the filling.

Slide the omelet onto a plate and repeat the process for the remaining omelet.

Serve and enjoy.

Smoked Salmon, Scrambled Eggs, and Spinach on English Muffins

For anyone who is sick, salmon is one of the most valuable protein sources to help recovery. It is vitamin and mineral-rich and can, thanks to its omega 3 fatty acids, assist the immune system to work more effectively.

Servings: 6

Total Time: 15mins

Ingredients:

- 1 tbsp olive oil
- 6 medium eggs
- ¼ tsp freshly ground black pepper
- 4 ounces smoked salmon (thinly sliced and diced)
- 4 ounces reduced-fat cream cheese (softened, and diced)
- 1 cup fresh spinach (chopped)
- 3 whole-grain English muffins (split and toasted)
- 1 tbsp chives (chopped)

Directions:

In a skillet over moderate heat, heat the oil.

In a bowl, combine the eggs with black pepper, and stir thoroughly with a whisk.

Pour the seasoned egg into the skillet, and cook until the mixture starts to thicken, for 30 seconds or so, while slowly stirring with a wooden spoon.

Fold in the salmon and diced cream cheese, and cook while mashing and constantly stirring with a wooden spoon.

Next, stir in the spinach, and cook for 2 minutes until the eggs are cooked and the spinach wilts.

Toast the muffins.

Top each toasted muffin half with ½ cup of the salmon-egg mixture.

Garnish with chopped chives and enjoy.

Spicy Sweet Potato Breakfast Hash

This spicy one-pan breakfast hash features chili peppers. Many people claim that eating spicy foods can cause a runny nose which can break up mucus and clear out the sinus passages. The foods, however, should be avoided by anyone suffering from an upset stomach.

Servings: 4

Total Time: 25mins

Ingredients:

- 1 tbsp olive oil
- 1 sweet potato (scrubbed and diced)
- ½ red onion (peeled and diced)
- 1 garlic clove (peeled and minced)
- 2 bell peppers (diced and seeded)
- 1 jalapeno (diced)
- 2 green onions (chopped)
- 1 tbsp fresh rosemary (chopped)
- 4 eggs

Directions:

Over moderate to high heat, in a skillet, heat the oil.

Add the diced sweet potato, cover with a lid, and cook for approximately 10 minutes while occasionally stirring until it starts to soften.

Add the red onion and garlic to the skillet, followed by the bell peppers and jalapeno.

Next, stir in the green onion and chopped rosemary.

Cover the pan with a lid. Then, cook for approximately 5 minutes until the potatoes are fork-tender.

Make 4 wells in the veggie mixture, in the center but not touching.

Crack 1 egg into each well. Cover the pan and cook for 3-5 minutes or until the eggs are cooked to your preferred liking.

Serve and enjoy.

Sweet Potato Toast

Did you know that one average size sweet potato provides over 100% of your recommended daily serving of vitamin A? This vitamin helps to regulate the immune system and protect against infection. So banish bread and instead opt for this veggie toast in the morning!

Servings: 2-4

Total Time: 25mins

Ingredients:

- 1 medium-large sweet potato
- Nut butter (to serve, optional)
- Fresh banana slices (to serve, optional)
- Cinnamon (to garnish, optional)

Directions:

Preheat the main oven to 400 degrees F. Using parchment paper, line a baking sheet.

Slice the ends of the sweet potato off and cut lengthwise into ½" thick slices.

In a single layer, place the slices on the parchment-lined sheet. There is no need to grease the paper.

Bake the potato slices in the preheated oven until fork-tender for around 18-20 minutes.

Remove from the oven, and serve warm, spread with nut butter, topped with fresh banana slices, and garnish with cinnamon.

Lite Bites and Mains

Asian-Style Fish Pie

Do you love fish? Are you searching for a comforting main that the whole family will enjoy? This nutrient-rich fish pie topped with sweet potatoes is the answer to all your weeknight dinner problems. Using coconut milk for the recipe rather than semi-skimmed milk will give the pie an Asian twist.

Servings: 4

Total Time: 1hr 10mins

Ingredients:

- 2 large sweet potatoes (peeled and cut into small size chunks)
- Salt and freshly ground black pepper (to season)

Sauce:

- 1 ounce butter
- 1 ounce flour
- 1¼ cups coconut milk (warm)
- Freshly squeezed juice of ½ lemon
- 1¼ cups vegetable stock
- 1 tsp wholegrain mustard
- 2 tbsp Parmesan cheese (grated and divided)
- 1 pound 2 ounces white fish fillets (e.g., cod, haddock, or hake, cut into bite-size chunks)
- 1 small fennel bulb (halved and thinly sliced)

Directions:

Preheat the main oven to 425 degrees F.

Add the sweet potatoes to a pan filled with water and boil until fork-tender for around 10 minutes. Drain and mash, seasoning with salt and black pepper, to taste.

In the meantime, prepare the white sauce. Over moderate heat, melt the butter in a pan.

Add the flour to the butter, and stir to create a paste, for 2 minutes.

Gradually, while constantly stirring, add the coconut milk to create a smooth consistency paste. Continue stirring for another 5-10 minutes until it thickens.

Add the fresh lemon juice, vegetable stock, and wholegrain mustard. Season the sauce to taste and fold through 1 tablespoon of grated Parmesan. Bring the sauce to a simmer, and cook for 60 seconds before removing the pan from the heat.

Add the fish to an ovenproof casserole dish. Distribute the sliced fennel evenly over the surface of the fish.

Pour the white sauce over the fish and top evenly with mashed sweet potato.

Scatter the remaining cheese over the surface.

Transfer the dish to a baking tray and place in the oven. Cook the pie for around 40-45 minutes until golden and cooked through.

Serve and enjoy.

Baked Applesauce Chicken

Whenever you were sick with stomach problems as a child, your mother most likely gave you applesauce. And nothing's changed! Apples contain antioxidants, fiber, and vitamins and are a great ingredient to combine with protein-rich lean chicken.

Servings: 2

Total Time: 25mins

Ingredients:

- 1 cup unsweetened applesauce
- A pinch of ground nutmeg
- ¼ tsp ground cinnamon
- 2 (4 ounces) skinless, boneless chicken breasts

Directions:

In a small skillet, stir the applesauce with nutmeg and cinnamon. Over low heat, bring to a boil; add a splash of water if needed to achieve your preferred consistency.

Cover the skillet with a lid and simmer for 3 minutes.

Add the chicken to a small casserole dish.

Pour the applesauce over the top. Bake in the oven at 350 degrees F until the chicken is cooked through. This step will take around 20-25 minutes.

Buddha Bowl with Carrot and Ginger Dressing

This bountiful Buddha bowl with its sweet and spicy dressing is sure to return the spring to your step!

Servings: 1

Total Time: 15mins

Ingredients:

Dressing:

- ⅓ cup extra-virgin olive oil
- ⅓ cup rice vinegar
- 2 large carrots (peeled and coarsely chopped)
- 2 tbsp fresh ginger (peeled and coarsely chopped)
- 2 tbsp fresh lime juice
- 1 tbsp + 1 tsp clear honey
- 1½ tsp toasted sesame oil
- ¼ tsp salt

Buddha Bowl:

- ¾ cup cooked brown rice
- ½ cup romaine lettuce (chopped)
- ½ cup sweet potatoes (cooked and cubed)
- ¼ cup carrots (diced small)
- 2 tbsp beets (cooked and cubed)
- 3 tbsp carrot and ginger dressing (see recipe)
- 1½ tbsp cilantro (chopped)

Directions:

For the dressing: In a food blender, combine the oil with rice vinegar, carrots, ginger, lime, juice honey, sesame oil, and salt. Process until smooth. Taste and add more salt if needed. To sweeten, add more honey.

Transfer to the fridge until needed. This recipe will yield around 1 ½ cups and can be stored, covered in the fridge for up to 14 days.

In a microwave-safe bowl, combine the brown rice with lettuce, sweet potatoes, carrots, and beets.

Microwave until just warm

Drizzle with carrot and ginger dressing, garnish with cilantro and enjoy.

Chicken and Turmeric Soup

This flu-fighting soup is sure to beat the sniffles! It has the right ingredients; garlic, ginger, chill, and turmeric, to help get you on the road to recovery.

Servings: 4

Total Time: 2hrs 15mins

Ingredients:

- 1 (3¼ pounds) whole chicken
- 1 small garlic head (horizontally sliced)
- 1 (2") ginger thumb (peeled and finely chopped)
- 1 tsp white peppercorns
- 1 tbsp coconut oil
- 1 long fresh red chili (finely chopped)
- 3 garlic cloves (peeled and finely chopped)
- 1 tbsp fresh ginger (peeled and finely chopped)
- 2 tsp ground turmeric
- 9 ounces canned coconut milk
- 7 ounces fresh sweet potatoes (peeled and spiralized)
- 1-2 tbsp tamari
- Freshly squeezed juice of 1 lime
- 4 lime wedges (to serve)
- Coriander sprigs (to garnish)

Directions:

Add the chicken to a 16-cup capacity stockpot. Pour in sufficient water to cover and over high heat, bring to a boil, skimming off any surface scum. Turn the heat down to low and add the head of garlic and chopped thumb of ginger, and white peppercorns. Simmer the mixture while occasionally skimming for 90 minutes until the chicken is tender.

Transfer the chicken to a plate and set aside to cool. Shred the chicken meat and discard any skin and bones.

Strain the resulting stock, discard the solids and set the liquid to one side.

Heat the coconut oil in a large pan.

Add the chili, finely chopped 3 cloves of garlic, 1 tablespoon of finely chopped ginger. Cook, while stirring for 2-3 minutes until aromatic. Stir in the turmeric.

Continue to cook the mixture for 60 seconds.

A little at a time, pour in the chicken stock, set aside in Step 3. Next, pour in the canned coconut milk. Simmer for 20 minutes or until slightly reduced.

Add the sweet potato spirals together with the shredded chicken and simmer for 4-6 minutes until the potato is tender.

Stir in the tamari (to taste) and fresh lime juice. Taste the soup and season with salt and pepper.

Garnish with coriander and few wedges of lime.

Serve and enjoy.

Chicken, Sweet Potato, and Coconut Stew

While some spicy foods can often help improve cough symptoms, they can also cause nausea or bloating. So provided you are not suffering from a digestive complaint, this spicy stew will tick all the taste boxes.

Servings: 6-8

Total Time: 50mins

Ingredients:

Spice Mixture:

- ¼ cup freshly squeezed orange juice
- 1 tbsp paprika
- 1 tsp ground cumin
- 1 tsp ground coriander
- 1 tsp ground turmeric
- ¼ tsp cayenne

Stew:

- 3 tbsp coconut oil (divided)
- 1 large onion (peeled and chopped)
- 1 (2") thumb fresh ginger (peeled and minced)
- 8 fresh garlic cloves (peeled and chopped)
- 1 (14½ ounces) can diced tomatoes in tomato juice
- ½ cup canned unsweetened coconut milk (shaken)
- 2 cups chicken broth
- Sea salt and freshly ground black pepper (as needed, to season)
- 1 pound sweet potatoes (peeled and cut into ½" pieces)
- 2 pounds boneless, skinless chicken thighs (patted dry and cut into bite-size pieces)
- Unsweetened coconut flakes (to garnish)

Directions:

First, prepare the spice mixture. In a bowl, combine the orange juice with paprika, ground cumin, coriander, turmeric, and cayenne.

For the stew: In a Dutch oven, add 2 tablespoons of coconut oil and heat through until hot.

Add the onions, stirring over moderate heat for 4 minutes until softened.

Next, add the ginger and garlic, continuing to stir for an additional 2 minutes. Finally, add the spice mixture from Step 1, stir thoroughly for 60 seconds.

Add the canned tomatoes along with their juices and coconut milk and frequently stir for around 2-3 minutes.

Pour in the chicken broth, and season with around ½ teaspoon sea salt. Bring the mixture to a simmer for 10 minutes.

Add the sweet potatoes while occasionally stirring for 20 minutes until tender. Taste and season with salt and black pepper.

While the stew is cooking, heat the remaining 1 tablespoon of coconut oil over moderate to high heat in a large pan.

Season the chicken with ½ teaspoon of sea salt and ¼ teaspoon of black pepper.

Add the chicken in a single layer to a pan, and brown on one side for 4 minutes. Flip the chicken over and brown for another 3 minutes. Do may need to do this in batches.

Add the browned chicken breasts to the stew, stirring to combine.

Garnish with coconut and serve.

Ginger and Garlic Brown Rice Pasta with Mixed Vegetables

Brown rice pasta is a valuable source of antioxidants, fiber, and minerals that can help optimize good health. In addition, its mild flavor is ideal for anyone recovering from an illness.

Servings: 6-8

Total Time: 15mins

Ingredients:

- 2 cups uncooked brown rice elbow pasta
- 1 tbsp coconut oil
- ½ small red onion (peeled and sliced)
- 2 tsp ginger paste
- 2 tsp garlic paste
- 1½ cups fresh Brussels sprouts (chopped)
- ½ cup red cabbage (chopped)
- ½ cup carrots (shredded)
- ½ medium sweet red pepper (chopped)
- ½ tsp salt
- ¼ tsp ground ancho chili pepper
- ¼ tsp coarsely ground black pepper
- 1 rotisserie chicken (skinned and shredded)
- 2 green onions (chopped)

Directions:

In a Dutch oven, cook the pasta according to the package instructions and until al dente.

In the meantime, in a large frying pan over moderate heat, warm the coconut oil.

Add the onion, ginger paste, and garlic paste to the pan and sauté for 2 minutes.

Stir in the sprouts, cabbage, carrots, red pepper, salt, chili pepper, and black pepper. Cook until the veggies are crisp-tender for approximately 4-6 minutes.

Add the shredded chicken to the Dutch oven, and heat through.

Drain the pasta, and set 1 cup of the pasta cooking liquid to one side.

Add the sprout mixture from Step 4, and toss to coat. Add sufficient pasta cooking water to moisten as needed.

Garnish with green onion and serve.

Mixed Bean and Avocado Tacos with Coconut Yoghurt Sauce

If you are feeling ill, then take-out tacos are a big no, no! But this homemade option is just as tasty and a lot better for you.

Servings: 2

Total Time: 1hr 20mns

Ingredients:

Pickled Red Onions (optional):

- 1 red onion (peeled and sliced)
- ½ tsp salt
- ½ tsp sugar
- 1 cup apple cider vinegar
- Salt and freshly ground black pepper (to season)

Tacos:

- 1 tbsp coconut oil
- 1 tsp cumin
- ¼ tsp smoked paprika
- 1 (14 ounces) can mixed beans (drained and rinsed)
- ½ cup peas
- ½ cup corn kernels
- 4 corn tortillas
- 4 tbsp store-bought hummus
- ½ cup grape tomatoes (halved)
- ½ ripe avocado (peeled, pitted, and sliced)
- 1 cup rocket leaves
- Fresh coriander leaves (to serve)
- Lime wedges (to serve)

Yogurt Sauce:

- 4 tbsp natural coconut flavor yogurt
- Freshly squeezed lime juice (to taste)
- 1 tbsp coriander leaves (finely chopped)

Directions:

First, prepare the pickled red onions. Add the onions to a Mason jar. To the jar, add the salt, sugar, and sufficient apple cider vinegar to cover. Stir well and transfer to the fridge for 60 minutes.

In a pan over moderate heat, heat the coconut oil.

To the pan, add the cumin and paprika and cook until fragrant.

Next, add the mixed beans, peas, and corn. Stir the mixture to evenly coat the beans and veggies in the spices. Cook for 1-2 minutes.

Warm the tortillas according to the package direction.

Spread the tortillas with hummus, top with the bean mixture. Next, add the halved tomatoes, rocket, avocado, and slices of red onion pickles (if using).

For the yogurt sauce dressing, combine the coconut yogurt with the fresh lime and coriander. Season the dressing to taste with salt and black pepper, and drizzle over the tacos.

Serve the tacos garnished with fresh coriander leaves, and serve with a wedge of fresh lime for squeezing.

Nut Roast

Nuts and seeds are rich in two nutrients needed for immune function; zinc and vitamin E. Cashews, almonds, and chia seeds are excellent choices for this main dish.

Servings: 6

Total Time: 50mins

Ingredients:

- 1 onion (peeled and diced)
- 2 garlic cloves (peeled and finely chopped)
- 2 tbsp olive oil
- 1½ cups mixed nuts of choice
- 1 cup fine wholemeal breadcrumbs
- 2 tbsp soy sauce
- 2 tsp dried herbs
- 1 cup vegetable stock
- 1 tbsp chia seeds
- 2 tbsp dried cranberries (chopped)

Directions:

Preheat the main oven to 355 degrees F.

In a frying pan, cook the onion and garlic in olive oil until beginning to brown.

In a food processor, on the pulse setting, process the nuts to a fine consistency.

In a bowl, combine the finely ground nuts with breadcrumbs, sautéed onion and garlic, soy sauce, dried herbs, stock, chia seeds, and cranberries.

Transfer the mixture to a lined loaf pan *8" x4" x2". Smooth the surface with a spatula. The mixture should come around ⅔ to the top of the pan.

Bake the nut roast for 30-40 minutes until the surface begins to brown.

Remove the nut roast from the oven and cool while still in the pan for 10 minutes.

Remove from the pan, peel away the baking paper, slice, and serve.

Pasta Carbonara with Greek Yogurt

Re-invent a family-favorite pasta dish with Greek yogurt! It is rich in probiotic cultures, which are essential for immune health, and unlike some ready-made versions, it doesn't contain fat-laden cream.

Servings: 4-6

Total Time: 15mins

Ingredients:

- 12 ounces uncooked whole-wheat linguine
- ½ cup plain Greek yogurt
- 6 ounces ham (chopped)
- ½ cup Parmesan cheese (finely grated)
- ½ tsp salt
- ½ tsp freshly ground black pepper
- 2 large eggs
- Parmesan cheese (finely grated, to garnish, optional)

Directions:

Cook the pasta according to the package instructions and until al dente. When it is ready to drain, remove 1-1½ cups of pasta cooking water, and set aside.

In the meantime, bring a pan of water to boil.

Pour the boiling water into a large bowl. Around 2-3 minutes before the pasta is cooked, pour the hot water out of the bowl. Its only purpose was to warm the bowl.

Add the Greek yogurt, ham, grated cheese, salt, and freshly ground black pepper to the warm bowl. Stir to combine and add the eggs, whisking with a fork.

Drain the pasta, set aside the water as instructed in Step 1, and add the hot pasta to the egg mixture.

Stir the pasta into the Greek yogurt sauce to coat. If the consistency is too thick, drizzle in a drop of water, 2 tablespoons at a time.

Serve garnished with grated cheese, and enjoy.

Salmon Oatmeal Hash

Due to its creamy consistency, this oatmeal hash is very easy to digest. It's kind to the throat too. The savory seafood version is ideal for serving to anyone whose appetite is starting to return.

Servings: 2

Total Time: 25mins

Ingredients:

- Nonstick cooking spray
- ½ yellow onion (peeled and chopped)
- ¼ cup uncooked steel-cut oats
- 1 cup water (boiling)
- 1 large zucchini (chopped)
- 1 cup cauliflower florets (finely chopped)
- 8 ounces cooked salmon
- Dill (to taste)
- Salt (to season)

Directions:

Spritz a large pan with nonstick cooking spray.

Cook the onion and the oats on moderate heat for around 2 minutes while frequently stirring.

Pour boiling water into the oat-onion mixture. Add the zucchini and cauliflower florets and simmer for around 15 minutes until the mixture is thickened slightly and the oats are chewy.

Remove the pan from the heat and set aside to thicken for another 2 minutes.

Fold in the cooked salmon, dill, and season with salt.

Sunflower Seed Burgers

Go bun-free and serve these meat-free burgers topped with mashed avocado and a fried egg.

Servings: 6

Total Time: 35mins

Ingredients:

- 1 cup sunflower seeds
- ½ cup carrots (grated)
- 1½ cups cooked browned rice
- ½ tsp sea salt
- 2 garlic cloves (peeled and minced)
- Olive oil (as needed)
- Avocado (peeled, pitted, and mashed, to serve, optional)
- 6 fried eggs (to serve, optional)

Directions:

Preheat the main oven to 400 degrees F. Using parchment paper, line a baking sheet.

In a food processor, process the sunflower seeds until coarsely ground. Remove from the processor and put to one side.

Combine the ground sunflower seeds, grated carrots, brown rice, sea salt, and garlic in the food processor. On the pulse setting, combine. You may need to add a drizzle of oil if the mixture is a little bit crumbly or dry.

Using clean hands, shape the sunflower seed mixture into 6 (3") patties.

Bake the burgers in the preheated oven, on the baking sheet, for 18-20 minutes. You will need to flip them over halfway through the cooking process.

Remove from the oven and cool slightly before serving topped with mashed avocado and a fried egg.

Tuna and Mushroom Egg Bake

Tuna is a nutritious fish packed with protein, vitamins, and healthy fats. It makes a healthy filling ingredient for this family-friendly pie.

Servings: 8

Total Time: 55mins

Ingredients:

Egg Mixture:

- 6 large free-range eggs
- ½ cup coconut milk
- ½ tsp cayenne
- ½ tsp garlic powder
- ¼ tsp Himalayan pink salt
- ½ tsp dried chilies

Filling:

- 1 medium onion (peeled and diced+
- 1½ cups chestnut cremini mushrooms (sliced)
- 1 cup red bell pepper (diced)
- 2 cups spring greens
- 1 (5 ounces) can wild-caught tuna in water (drained)
- ¼ tsp Himalayan pink salt
- ½ tsp black pepper

Directions:

Preheat the main oven to 350 degrees F.

For the egg mixture: Break the eggs into a bowl. Add the coconut milk, cayenne, garlic powder, pink salt, and dried chilies.

For the filling: In an oven-safe pot, on low to moderate heat, sauté the onion and mushrooms for 5-8 minutes until the mushrooms are soft and the onions translucent.

Add the bell peppers, and cook for another 3-4 minutes.

Add the greens, and cook until vivid green and wilted slightly.

Stir in the tuna, and combine. Season with salt and black pepper.

Finally, add the egg mixture.

Transfer the oven-safe dish to the oven. Cook for 40-45 minutes or until the egg is cooked through and the surface of the bake is crisp and golden.

Serve and enjoy.

Turkey and Mixed Mushroom Pie

Whether you are already feeling under the weather or recovering from an illness, this turkey and mushroom pie is the quintessential comfort food.

Servings: 4

Total Time: 1hr

Ingredients:

- 2 tsp rapeseed oil
- 2 onions (peeled and thinly sliced)
- 1 (11 ounces) package turkey breast (cut into cubes)
- 2 garlic cloves (peeled and sliced)
- 8 ounces mushrooms (sliced)
- 3½ ounces whole button mushrooms
- 1 tsp Dijon mustard
- 1 tsp dried thyme
- 1 tbsp plain flour
- 1 reduced-salt chicken stock cube
- 13½ ounces water (boiling, for stock)
- 3 store-bought filo pastry sheets
- Nonstick cooking oil spray

Directions:

Preheat the main oven to 350 degrees F.

Add the rapeseed oil to a pan.

Add the onions to the pan and cook while occasionally stirring for 5 minutes or until starting to brown.

Add the cubed turkey, and while frequently stirring, cook for another 4-5 minutes.

Next, add the garlic, sliced mushrooms, and whole button mushrooms, and cook for another 5 minutes while frequently stirring.

Stir in the mustard, dried thyme, and flour, making sure the mixture is combined and lump-free.

Slowly stir in the stock, bring to a boil, then reduce the heat.

Cover the pan with a lid and while occasionally stirring, simmer for 10 minutes.

Transfer the turkey mixture to a casserole dish, and spritz the pastry sheets with nonstick cooking spray. Place 1 pastry sheet on top of the turn, folding it. Add a second sheet and spritz with spray, and then add the third and final sheet, making folds across the surface.

Spritz the surface with nonstick cooking spray and bake in the preheated oven until golden.

Remove from the oven and enjoy with your favorite veggies.

Sweet Treats and Desserts

Applesauce Bars

Applesauce, like apples, is a healthy addition to your diet. It is a valuable source of vitamin C and fiber.

Servings: 20

Total Time: 45mins

Ingredients:

- ¼ cup butter (room temperature)
- ⅔ cup brown sugar
- 1 egg
- 1 cup applesauce
- 1 cup all-purpose flour
- 1 tsp bicarbonate of soda
- ½ tsp salt
- 1 tsp pumpkin pie spice
- 1½ cups confectioners' sugar
- 3 tbsp margarine (melted)
- 1 tbsp milk
- 1 tsp vanilla extract

Directions:

Preheat the main oven to 350 degrees F. Grease a 9x13" baking pan.

In a bowl, mix the butter with brown sugar and egg until silky smooth. Stir in the applesauce.

Combine the flour, bicarbonate of soda, salt, and pumpkin pie spice. Stir into the butter-applesauce mixture until thoroughly blended. Spread the mixture evenly into the baking pan.

Bake in the oven for 25 minutes, until golden around the edges. Allow to cool in the pan set over a wire baking rack.

In a small bowl, combine the confectioners' sugar with margarine. Stir in the milk and vanilla extract until silky smooth. Spread the mixture over the now cooled bars before slicing into squares.

Baked Egg Custard

Are you under the weather and feeling a little sorry for yourself? This traditional baked egg custard is the ultimate comfort food. Enjoy on its own or top with your favorite fruits.

Servings: 4

Total Time: 45mins

Ingredients:

- 3 whole eggs
- 1 egg yolk
- 1 tsp vanilla extract
- 15¼ ounces half milk and half cream
- 2 ounces caster sugar
- Freshly grated nutmeg (to dust)

Directions:

Preheat the main oven to 335 degrees F.

In a bowl, lightly beat the whole eggs with the egg yolk and vanilla extract.

Add the half milk-cream to a pan together with the sugar, and stir to dissolve. Heat the mixture to just below boiling point. Pour the cream mixture onto the beaten egg mixture and stir to incorporate.

Strain the mixture through a sieve into a baking dish of 4-cup capacity.

Place the dish in a pan half-filled with hot water.

Scatter nutmeg over the surface of the egg custard and bake in the oven for approximately 30-35 minutes. The egg custard will slightly wobble.

Serve warm or chilled, and enjoy.

Banana Cream Pie

Fight the flu with potassium-rich bananas! Better yet, the whole family can tuck into this creamy pie whether they are fighting fit or under the weather.

Servings: 6-8

Total Time: 2hrs 15mins

Ingredients:

- Dough for single-crust pie
- ¾ cup sugar
- ⅓ cup all-purpose flour
- ¼ tsp salt
- 2 cups whole milk
- 6 ounces egg yolks (light beaten, room temperature)*
- 2 tbsp butter
- 1 tsp vanilla extract
- 3 medium firm bananas (peeled)
- Whipped cream (to serve, optional)

Directions:

On a lightly floured work surface, roll the dough out to an ⅛" thick circle. Transfer the dough to a 9" pie plate. Trim the dough, so it is ½" beyond the plate's rim and flute the edge. Transfer to the fridge for 30 minutes to chill.

Preheat the main oven to 425 degrees F.

Using a double thickness of aluminum foil, line the crust. Fill the crust with baking beans. Bake the crust in the lower part of the oven rack for 20-25 minutes, until the bottom is golden brown. Remove the foil and beans and bake for another 3-6 minutes, until the bottom is golden. Set aside to cool on a wire baking rack.

In the meantime, in a pan, combine the sugar, flour, and salt. Next, pour in the milk and mix thoroughly.

Cook the mixture over moderate to high heat until the mixture is bubbly and thickened. Cook while stirring for another 2 minutes.

Remove the pan from the heat.

Stir in a small amount into the egg yolks, and return all to the pan. Bring to a gentle boil, and while stirring, cook for 2 minutes. Remove the pan from the heat.

Add the butter and vanilla extract, and allow to cool slightly.

Slice the bananas and arrange them on the crust.

Pour the filling over the bananas, and on a wire baking rack, cool for 60 minutes.

Store the pie in the fridge.

Serve with optional whipped cream and enjoy.

*For this recipe the amount should be precise but you will need around 3 large eggs to achieve the weight measurement

Berry and Greek Yogurt Swirls

Cool and creamy, these Greek yogurt and honey popsicles are berry-nice for sore throats!

Servings: 10

Total Time: 2hrs 15mins

Ingredients:

- 2½ cups fat-free Greek yogurt
- 1 cup mixed fresh berries of choice
- ¼ cup water
- 2 tbsp sugar

Directions:

Fill 10 (3 ounces) plastic or paper cups with approximately ¼ cup each of Greek yogurt.

In a food processor, combine the berries, water, and sugar. On the pulse setting, process until finely chopped.

Spoon 1 ½ tablespoons of the berry mixture into each cup. Using a popsicle stick, stir gently to swirl.

Top each cup with foil, insert a popsicle stick through the foil.

Transfer to the freezer to set.

Chocolate Banana Chia Seed Pudding

This pudding is a real pick-me-up. Chia seeds contain the right sort of fiber and support the body's waste disposal system, making them a great addition to all sorts of recipes, including the pudding.

Servings: 1

Total Time: 1hr 5mins

Ingredients:

- ¾ cup 2% milk
- 1 tbsp chia seeds
- 1 tsp unsweetened cocoa powder
- ½ tsp cinnamon
- ½ banana (peeled and sliced)
- 1 tsp maple syrup

Directions:

In a tall glass or dessert bowl, combine the milk, chia seeds, cocoa powder, cinnamon, bananas, and maple syrup. Stir to incorporate, and place in the fridge for 1-8 hours.

Serve and enjoy.

Chocolate Beet Cake

If you have a family member who isn't a big fan of nutrient-rich beets, this moist chocolate cake with its hidden veggie is the way to go.

Servings: 12-16

Total Time: 1hr 20mins

Ingredients:

- 2 cups beets (cooked and cooled)
- Nonstick cooking spray
- Cocoa powder (to dust)
- ½ cup unsalted butter (melted and cooled slightly)
- ½ cup olive oil
- ½ cup dark brown sugar
- ½ cup granulated sugar
- ½ cup honey
- 3 medium eggs (room temperature)
- 1 tsp pure vanilla extract
- 2 cups cake flour
- ¾ cup unsweetened cocoa powder
- 2 tsp bicarbonate of soda
- A pinch of salt
- Chocolate buttercream or frosting (prepared)

Directions:

Grate the cooled beets until you yield 2 loosely packed cups.

Place a colander over a large mixing bowl. Transfer the grated beets to the colander, and allow them to drain naturally. No need to use wring, press, or use kitchen paper.

Preheat the main oven to 350 degrees F. Spritz 2 (9") circular cake pans with nonstick cooking spray. Lightly dust the pans with cocoa powder, and put to one side.

In a bowl, whisk the butter, oil, brown sugar, granulated sugar, and honey until combined thoroughly.

Add the eggs and vanilla extract and stir to incorporate.

In a separate bowl, whisk the flour, cocoa powder, and bicarbonate of soda and salt.

Slowly add the dry ingredients to the wet ingredients, and stir well to combine.

Add the grated beets, and stir well to incorporate.

Transfer the batter to the prepared cake pan, and with a rubber spatula, smooth over the surface.

One at a time, bake each cake for 25 minutes until the center of the cakes are springy to the touch. Allow the cakes to cool while in the pan for 20-30 minutes.

Loosen the cakes from the pan, using a blunt knife, and invert onto a wire baking rack.

Allow the cakes to cool completely,

Using a serrated knife, slice a thin layer off the surface of each cake so they are flat and easy to stack.

Place the first cake layer on a plate, and cover with your favorite chocolate buttercream or frosting.

Cover the frosting with the second cake layer, and enjoy.

Coco Lemon Bliss Balls

Sugar-laden candies aren't a good idea for anyone suffering from a cold or flu. Once you are on the road to recovery, though, these pop-in-the-mouth coconut and lemon bliss balls sweetened with maple syrup are sheer bliss in every bite!

Servings: 12

Total Time: 40mins

Ingredients:

- 2¼ cups desiccated coconut
- Zest of 1 medium-large lemon
- Freshly squeezed juice of ½ lemon
- 2 tbsp coconut cream (chilled)
- 2 tbsp coconut water
- 3 tbsp maple syrup

Directions:

Using parchment paper, line a cookie sheet. Set to one side.

Add the desiccated coconut, lemon zest, fresh lemon juice, coconut cream, coconut water, and maple syrup to a food processor.

On the pulse setting, pulse 2-3 times to combine ingredients. Next, process on high speed until combined and the mixture is starting to stick together.

In 1-2 tablespoonful amounts, create small-size round balls. If the mixture doesn't hold its shape, you may want to add additional desiccated coconut.

Arrange the balls on the prepared cookie sheet and place in the fridge for 30 minutes.

Store in an airtight container, in the fridge, for up to 7 days.

Golden Rice Pudding with Turmeric and Coconut Milk

When you are under the weather, a bowl of this creamy rice pudding will come to the rescue.

Servings: 2

Total Time: 45mins

Ingredients:

- 3½ ounces short-grain rice
- 2 cups water
- 1 tsp ground turmeric
- A dash of black pepper
- ⅘ cup canned full-fat coconut milk
- 1 tbsp coconut sugar
- 1 tsp vanilla extract
- Bananas slices (to serve)
- Maple syrup (to sweeten)

Directions:

Cook the short-grain rice in the water, turmeric and black pepper for approximately 35 minutes or until cooked. You may need to add a splash more water if needed.

When the rice is ready, strain and return to the pan.

Pour in the coconut milk and add the coconut sugar and vanilla. Cook for another 10 minutes, while occasionally stirring until the mixture thickens. For a creamier consistency, add more coconut milk.

Top with fresh slices of banana and a spoonful of maple syrup.

Greek Yogurt Cheesecake

Greek yogurt is an excellent source of calcium and contains probiotics, which support a healthy bacterial balance in the gut. This homemade cheesecake is way better than any you can buy in a bakery or store.

Servings: 6-8

Total Time: 10hrs

Ingredients:

- 1½ cups Greek yogurt
- ½ cup cream cheese (softened)
- ¼ tsp salt
- 1½ tsp pure vanilla extract
- ½ tbsp lemon juice
- ½ cup pure maple syrup
- 1 tbsp cornstarch
- 1 (9") store-bought prepared pie crust

Directions:

Preheat the main oven to 350 degrees F.

In a food blender, combine Greek yogurt, cream cheese, salt, vanilla extract, lemon juice, maple syrup, and cornstarch.

Pour the smooth mixture into the pie crust.

Bake in the oven for 50 minutes, then take out of the oven. The cheesecake will appear underdone. Allow to cool for 60 minutes before transferring, uncovered to the fridge, to set. This will take around 8 hours.

Remove from the fridge. When firm, slice and enjoy.

Key Lime Pie Fro Yo

When you are feeling under the weather, who doesn't love a big comforting bowl of ice cream? But instead of reaching for the store-bought frozen treat, whip up a batch of fro yo. It is far better for your digestive health and can help boost the immune system.

Servings: 8

Total Time: 35mins

Ingredients:

- 32 ounces low-fat plain yogurt
- 1 (14 ounces) can fat-free sweetened condensed milk
- 1 tsp vanilla extract
- 1 cup fresh lime juice
- Zest of 1 lime

Directions:

In an ice cream maker, combine the yogurt, milk, vanilla extract, lime juice, and zest, and freeze according to the manufacturer's instructions.

Serve as soft serve, and enjoy.

Lemon Oatmeal Cookies

When you don't feel like a meal but want something to nibble on, these lemon oatmeal cookies will hit the spot!

Servings: 54

Total Time: 40mins

Ingredients:

- 1 cup butter-flavored shortening
- 3 ounces cream cheese (softened)
- 1¼ cups sugar
- 1 large egg yolk
- 2 tsp grated lemon zest
- 1 tsp lemon extract
- 1⅓ cups all-purpose flour
- 1⅓ cups quick-cooking oats
- ½ tsp salt

Topping:

- 1 large egg
- 1 large egg white
- Sugar (as needed)
- ½ cup sliced almonds

Directions:

In a bowl, cream the shortening, cream cheese, and sugar until fluffy and light. Beat in the egg yolk, lemon zest, and lemon extract.

Combine the flour, quick-cook oats, and salt and a little at a time, add to the creamed mixture, and stir well.

In heaped teaspoonfuls, approximately 2" apart, drop the mixture onto greased baking sheets.

In a small bowl, beat the egg and egg white, and brush all over the dough.

Scatter sugar and sliced almonds over the top.

Bake in the oven at 350 degrees F, for 10-12 minutes, until the edges are browned lightly.

Remove from the oven and allow to cool on wire baking racks.

Spiced Sugar Candy

Soothing ginger and cinnamon combine with throat-happy honey to create this spiced sugar candy. So if you aren't up to a trip to the pharmacy or store, whip up a batch of the spiced sugar candy.

Servings: 20-25

Total Time: 15mins

Ingredients:

- ½ cup brown sugar
- 2 tbsp honey
- ½ tsp ginger
- ½ tsp freshly ground black pepper
- ¼ tsp cinnamon
- ¼ tsp cayenne pepper

Directions:

In a small pan, melt the sugar with the honey until golden brown.

Add the ginger, black pepper, cinnamon, and cayenne pepper, and mix well to combine.

Using a spoon, drop the candy mixture onto a sheet of greaseproof paper, and set aside to cool and set. Aim to yield around 20-25 candies.

Watermelon and Coconut Water Popsicles

Coconut water contains natural electrolytes, such as manganese, sodium, and potassium. So if you are looking to rehydrate, these popsicles are a welcome treat.

Servings: 6-8

Total Time: 3hrs

Ingredients:

- 4 cups watermelon chunks (peeled and seeded)
- ½ cup coconut water
- Freshly squeezed juice of 1 fresh lime
- 2 tbsp agave nectar

Directions:

In a food blender, combine the watermelon, coconut water, fresh lime juice, and agave nectar. Puree the mixture until smooth.

Pour the mixture into popsicle molds and transfer to the freezer until solid.

Author's Afterthoughts

I would like to express my deepest thanks to you, the reader, for making this investment in one my books. I cherish the thought of bringing the love of cooking into your home.

With so much choice out there, I am grateful you decided to Purch this book and read it from beginning to end.

Please let me know by submitting an Amazon review if you enjoyed this book and found it contained valuable information to help you in your culinary endeavors. Please take a few minutes to express your opinion freely and honestly. This will help others make an informed decision on purchasing and provide me with valuable feedback.

Thank you for taking the time to review!

Christina Tosch

About the Author

Christina Tosch is a successful chef and renowned cookbook author from Long Grove, Illinois. She majored in Liberal Arts at Trinity International University and decided to pursue her passion of cooking when she applied to the world renowned Le Cordon Bleu culinary school in Paris, France. The school was lucky to recognize the immense talent of this chef and she excelled in her courses, particularly Haute Cuisine. This skill was recognized and rewarded by several highly regarded Chicago restaurants, where she was offered the prestigious position of head chef.

Christina and her family live in a spacious home in the Chicago area and she loves to grow her own vegetables and herbs in the garden she lovingly cultivates on her sprawling estate. Her and her husband have two beautiful children, 3 cats, 2 dogs and a parakeet they call Jasper. When Christina is not hard at work creating beautiful meals for Chicago's elite, she is hard at work writing engaging e-books of which she has sold over 1500.

Make sure to keep an eye out for her latest books that offer helpful tips, clear instructions and witty anecdotes that will bring a smile to your face as you read!

Printed in Great Britain
by Amazon

29095841R00062